4 Indisputable Reasons to Plan

by Ben Gothard,
Founder & CEO of Gothard Enterprises LLC
Author of CEO at 20: A Little Book for Big Dreams

4 Indisputable Reasons to Plan

Do you want to achieve greatness but don't know how to do it? If so, you're not alone. Many people have powerful goals, such as climbing Mt. Everest, starting a school, getting a degree, or finding that special someone with whom to share a lifetime. While many people want to achieve greatness, most never do. One of the most common reasons why is that most people fail to plan for success! Without a plan, you will be aimlessly moving through life. You may achieve some success, but you will more than likely never be able to accomplish massive "life goals."

The people who have changed the world for the better are the people who have planned on doing so! They took their futures into their own hands, decided on a course of action and figured out what steps they needed to take in order to make their dreams a reality. Not only can you follow in the footsteps of some of the greatest movers and shifters in history, but, if you so choose to, you can even carve a completely new path to success. How? Planning. In this book, I will give you 4 indisputable reasons to plan.

Direction

Have you ever had to get somewhere without knowing where to go? It is frustrating! You may not have thought about it in this way before, but you were trying to achieve your goal without direction. If you don't have a clear path laid out in front of you, it is difficult to achieve something. Planning allows you to create that path for yourself and give direction to your efforts.

Back in the BC era, pirates and sailors would use landmarks and the position of the moon, sun and stars to figure out where they were and in which direction they were traveling. However, they couldn't take long journeys away from the land without risk of getting lost at sea. This was a huge problem until the compass was invented in China sometime in the 1st century AD. They found out that lodestone could be suspended and would naturally point to the magnetic poles. This miracle invention gave seafarers direction even when it was cloudy or there were no landmarks, and led to the Age of Exploration. While direction to the sailor meant freedom to roam the vast oceans, direction to your plan means freedom to pursue anything that you choose. When you have a plan with direction, you can make incredible things happen.

Take PayPal for example. Founders Peter Thiel and Elon Musk had two separate companies in the 1990's, Confinity and X.com, which both were involved in money transfer. The two joined forces, focusing on a few different services including PayPal. All the while, Musk knew the direction he wanted to take the company was in the world of virtual payments. After riding ups and downs for a few years, Musk and Thiel did away with everything except for PayPal.

They stayed true to their goal and planned to dominate the money service business. They had direction, and a hunch that their company was going to take the world by storm. In early 2002, the company went public, drawing in over $61 million, and by July PayPal was acquired by eBay for $1.5 billion. Fast forward to 2016, and PayPal is generating over $9.24 billion in annual revenue with over $280 billion in annual payment volume. The founders had a plan with direction. This gave them the guidance that they needed to succeed by laying out a clear path to success.

However, not all entrepreneurs start out with a plan that gives them direction. Some find success accidentally and then take it to the next level with a plan. Take entrepreneur and philanthropist Pierre Morad Omidyar, the founder of eBay, for example. Born 1967 in Paris, France, Omidyar didn't set out to become a wildly successful Internet tycoon. He started on his journey at 14 when he built his first computer program to catalog books for the school library. After getting a computer science degree from Tufts in 1988, he worked on a few different projects until 1995, when his life would change forever.

That summer, Omidyar built code for a section of his personal website called Auction Web where he let people put up items for auction. In a very short amount of time, he had so many people buying and selling on his site that he had to create an entirely new site just for this auction marketplace. He called it eBay, and this was the beginning of the ecommerce giant that has revolutionized the entire industry. Omidyar figured out that the best way to monetize his online marketplace was to charge a listing fee of $2 or less and take a percentage of the sale. Within nine months of the first auction on his site, he quit everything else and fully devoted himself to eBay.

Once he decided to get serious about this venture of his, he immediately started planning because he knew that he needed direction. By 1998, he already had appointed a CEO (Meg Whitman) who would help him reach the vision he had planned – to revolutionize the ecommerce industry. Under Whitman's direction, eBay continued to expand to Australia, Canada, Germany, Japan and the United Kingdom through site launches, joint ventures and acquisitions. With his plan and direction, Omidyar's company had over 2.1 million users and $750 million in revenue at the end of 1998. As of 2016, eBay has over 165 million registered users, a market capitalization of $27.9 billion, and continues to be a leader in ecommerce. By maintaining its direction and following the plan laid out by Omidyar so many years ago, eBay is an economic behemoth that shows no signs of going anywhere anytime soon.

Another shining example of the benefits of planning is Joe Coulombe, founder of Trader Joe's. The business began in 1958 in Los Angeles as a local chain of *Pronto Market* stores. However, Coulombe quickly realized that he couldn't and didn't want to compete with the 7-Eleven chain that was so similar. So he hit the drawing boards again and started brainstorming. He came up with the South Seas motif in the Caribbean, took notes from Trader Vic's, and noticed that Americans weren't getting the fresh and exotic food or wine that they wanted from supermarkets. With all of this information, he had a new plan made and a better direction to go towards. Coulombe opened his first Trader Joe's in 1967, and after opening up more than 20 locations, sold out for a pretty penny (albeit he has never publically said how much) to German grocery tycoon Theo Albrecht.

While the story of Coulombe is a short one, he set up Trader Joe's for a massive amount of future success through his successful planning and brilliant direction. From 1990 to 2001, Trader Joe's quintupled the number of its stores and multiplied its profits by ten. As of 2015, it is estimated that the grocery store did over $13 billion in sales with 460 locations and over 38,000 employees. It all started with a plan, which gave the business the direction it needed to become a superstar in the retail game.

When you plan, you give yourself direction by laying out a clear path to success.

Freedom

Are there things in your life that you have to do that you would prefer not to? Perhaps your boss says that you have to show up to work at a certain time or you have too many responsibilities that you can't make any decisions for yourself. Whatever the reason is, it is frustrating! If you know this feeling, then you have been struggling with a lack of freedom. If you don't plan out your own path, somebody else will do it for you. Planning allows you to create that path for yourself and gives you the freedom to spend time doing what you actually care about doing.

Freedom was one of the biggest reasons that I decided to devote my life to entrepreneurship. To me, the freedom to do what I want whenever I want to is worth more than any amount of money. The idea of having to work for somebody else makes me want to cringe, and I refuse to let my "boss" tell me when to show up to work. I plan to the best of my abilities because I know that if I don't, somebody else will plan it for me.

Freedom is not only a reason to plan, but also a fundamental human right. When, in the late 1700's, Great Britain restricted enough freedoms of the people of the colonies, they revolted and formed the United States of America. The document that separated the two countries is known as the Declaration of Independence! It reads as follows: "We hold these truths to be self-evident, that all men are created equal, that they are endowed by their Creator with certain unalienable Rights, that among these are Life, Liberty and the pursuit of Happiness." One of the three most basic rights is liberty!

The people of America were discontented with their former ruler, and they created a Constitution in addition to the Declaration so that the rules of this new nation could be written down into history. True to their nature, the newly emancipated states called for even *more* freedom once the Constitution was ratified, so a Bill of Rights was written. The very first Amendment states "Congress shall make no law respecting an establishment of religion, or prohibiting the free exercise thereof; or abridging the freedom of speech, or of the press; or the right of the people peaceably to assemble, and to petition the government for a redress of grievances."

If freedom could provoke an entire nation to break away from its mother country, than it can and certainly should be reason enough for you to plan. By planning your life out, even in the least detail, you give yourself the freedom to choose how you will spend your time; you can waste it, invest it, or use it in whatever way you like. The important thing is that you are making the decision. Nobody is making it for you.

Just because you have the freedom to make your own decisions doesn't mean you will be successful immediately, however. Take entrepreneurs John Ferolito and Don Vultaggio, the guys who launched AriZona Green Tea. The two high school buddies went into business together in the early 1970's, and they planned to make a name for themselves in the beverage wholesaling game. They started their journey by delivering cheap bear and soda to lower income areas in Brooklyn. After racking up enough business to own a small fleet of delivery trucks, they wanted to try their hands at making their own product. Although not wildly successful with their first beverage, flavored seltzer water, the friends started gaining some momentum after releasing their malt liquor, Midnight Dragon. Despite only being available in New York City, the entrepreneurs had estimated sales of over a million cases by 1988. After releasing one more malt liquor brand, Crazy Horse, they reached a plateau of $10 million in annual revenues in 1992.

The end of 1992 was when it all changed. Ferolito and Vultaggio decided it was time to enter a new market. After seeing the success of rival Snapple in the tea industry, they planned their next move. Because they had taken the time to reevaluate their plan and take full advantage of the freedom to choose their own path, they successfully launched AriZona Green Tea. As opposed to Snapple's 16-oz can, AriZona Green Tea was available in 24-oz containers with the same bright colors that the two had seen worked so well in Brooklyn's inner city. They sold more than ten million cases in 1993, spiking their revenues from $10 million in 1992 to over $130 million in 1993. After bringing in a point man for expansion, sales jumped up to $300 million in 1994 and $355 in 1995.

Today, legal battles between the high school friends and Ferolito's leave of the company has left the business stagnant. However, their rise to glory serves as a shining example of the freedom that planning can give you. They started off as distributors, pivoted into creating their own products, and slowly wormed their way from alcoholic beverages to tea. If they hadn't planned their business moves before they were made, they probably wouldn't have been able to so seamlessly alter their product offerings. Because they planned, they gave themselves the freedom to carve their own path to being a global phenomenon.

When you plan, you gain the freedom to choose your own path to success.

Power

When you learn about the biggest businesses on the globe, the real movers and shifters of the economic landscape, you probably noticed something that they all had in common. They make things happen. Regardless of the obstacles in front of them, the difficulties that they face, and the strength of their competitors, the most successful people on the planet get what they need to get done, done. How can this be explained? Simply put, they have power. They have the authority to put things in motion and make real change. With this amount of power and influence, do you think that these entrepreneurial all-stars make global change on a whim? Absolutely NOT!! They have enormously complex and far-reaching plans.

Think about the last time you accomplished something meaningful. Whether it was building a shed in your backyard or graduating from college or getting a promotion, I'd be willing to bet that you didn't randomly accomplish such a feat in a single day. In fact, you were probably working at it diligently for an extended period of time. If you did, then you planned to do so, and because of that planning, you gave yourself the ability and power to make that goal a reality. Planning gives you the power to accomplish big things by breaking them down into smaller, more manageable tasks. This power, believe it or not, is the same power that the movers and shifters of the world tap into in order to accomplish their goals.

In reality, there is little difference between you and them. One of the only stark contrasts is the power they give themselves through furiously planning. As Steve Jobs, late CEO of Apple says, "Those who are crazy enough to think they can change the world usually do." In fact, the story of Jobs and his partner, Steve Wozniak, is a perfect example of the power of planning. These two planned to impact society in a way that would change the way people perceived how the world worked. In the late 1970's, when the personal computer revolution was starting to catch fire, Wozniak built the Apple I as a way for the little man to take on a corporation. The two planned to give individuals machines that would let anyone stand toe to toe with vastly greater resourced companies.

Because they planned so ferociously and kept on thinking bigger, they were able to give themselves power. They didn't have a massive budget or serious connections, yet they made millions in their first year of business, $10 million in year two, and reached the billion-dollar status in just six years. If they hadn't planned so well in those formative years, chances are nobody would know what an iPhone was today.

Not all planners become billionaires, but everyone who has been successful has been a skilled planner. In Dr. Thomas J. Stanley's book, *The Millionaire Mind*, over 700 millionaires were studied in order to understand what made them successful. In one particular area of the study, the author asked the millionaires what actions or processes they used in order to eliminate any fears and worries they had on their journey to success. Over 87% said that planning was important. Stanley went on to recount the following story:

"Mr. Benjamin paid all of his children's tuition. His daughter and sons all attended private elementary and high schools and prestigious private colleges, medical colleges, and graduate schools. Mr. Benjamin paid for all of it – room, board, tuition, books and related expenses. Who is this man who demonstrated the ability to fund these enormous tuition bills – a highly paid physician or perhaps CEO of a major public corporation?"

The author went on to say that Mr. Benjamin was a school-bus driver, yet he sent his children to private college, medical school, and graduate school. How did he do it? You guessed it! He planned. Mr. Benjamin knew early on that his children were smart, and wanted to give them the very best education that he possibly could. As such, Mr. Benjamin planned to save up enough money to send them to the very best schools that he could. He rigorously designed his days to maximize the amount of self-improvement he could get in, and he started building up knowledge of investing. He learned about bonds, bills, stocks, real estate, and commodities, and eventually decided that he was going to become a serious stock investor.

With his plan in mind, he gave himself the power to dominate his chosen avocation while he drove the bus everyday. The result of his forethought was that he retired with a net worth in excess of $3 million *after* "sending his children to the finest, most expensive schools in America." The lesson to be learned is that even a bus driver who plans can give himself enough power to become successful. He was a long-term investor with a long-term plan. Mr. Benjamin is a shining example of the power that you can infuse into your life through successful planning. Follow in his footsteps, and you too can become successful.

When you plan, you give yourself the power to change the world.

Balance

Do you ever feel like you don't have any work-life balance? Sometimes you get burnt out at work, and other times you can barely be found in the office? Finding that perfect mixture of accomplishing your professional goals and spending time enjoying your personal life is CRITICAL to achieving massive success in your life. If you spend too much time doing one or the other, you will start to falter. For example, if you spend all of your time at work and don't make time for your family, you will miss out on a lot of important events like birthdays, anniversaries, or sports games, potentially damaging relationships with those whom you should be closest to. On the other hand, if you spend all of your time partying or enjoying your personal life, you won't ever be able to accomplish anything meaningful in your life and probably run out of money.

Needless to say, without a good balance of work and play, you are going to run into trouble. So how do you make sure that you can both? You plan! By making time in your calendar for the gym, family, and yourself, you can create work life balance. I struggle with this one too. As a 22 year old Entrepreneur, CEO, Author, and student, I find myself wearing a lot of different hats throughout the day. Whether it is going to meetings, talking to clients, writing, or studying for an exam, there are any number of things that eat away at my schedule. If I don't force myself to eat, go to the gym, and hang out with friends, I'll forget to do it. However, I have made it a priority to put in appointments in my calendar to go work out and eat. I find that if I treat it like a meeting, I am a lot more likely to make it a priority.

Not only can I make sure to find more balance in my life through planning, but I find that a healthy does of work and play actually improves my ability to perform at work and enjoy experiences in my personal life. If I spend too much time working, then the quality of my work and my focus starts to dip. On the other hand, if I spend too much time being unproductive, then I feel like I'm wasting time!

In fact, there are plenty of other entrepreneurs whose work life balance has been incredibly crucial to their success. Take Hannah Loaring for example. In 2010, the thirty year old was at rock bottom with $24,000 in debt and no semblance of a good work life balance.

However, she decided to make a change and make a plan so that she could start working to live, instead of having to live to work. In order to pay off her massive debt, she took on four jobs as a freelance designer, babysitter, waitress, and shop assistant. She worked 80 to 100 hours a week for 18 months until she had saved up double what she owed.

By thirty-three, she was an award winning blogger, world traveler, co-founder of her own graphic and web design business, Further Bound. Because she made a plan to reach specific goals (like getting out of debt), she was able to achieve the work life balance she so desperately desired. Now she travels at her leisure for fun, works remotely, and even has time to write books.

There are plenty of entrepreneurs who have attested to the importance of work life balance. Alex Chaidaroglou, CEO and cofounder of Altosight LTD, said, "We are doing a disservice to our clients, team and product if we burn out." He knows that if he isn't operating at a very high level, the people around him are the ones who suffer. Josh Steimle, Founder & CEO of MWI, told his team "This business matters a lot to me, but my family comes first, and I hope your families come before your job." Whether it be for your business or your team, you as an entrepreneur need some sort of balance in your life to stay at the top of your game. Sid Bharath, VP of Growth at Thinkific, said, "We don't realize that the more we work, the higher the chances of us running out of creative ideas and burning out." Billionaire Richard Branson once wrote "My family is the center of my life, so wherever I am in the world, when I have a few minutes, I talk to my wife and kids." From youngsters to experienced billionaires, entrepreneurs around the world recognize how importance work life balance is, and planning is the vehicle that you can use to accomplish that balance.

When you plan, you allow yourself to find balance in order to accomplish your professional goals and enjoy your personal life.

Tying It All Together

At the end of the day, planning is a crucial element of success. Whether you want it to or not, time is going to pass. The only thing that you can control is what you do in the time that you are given. By planning, you maximize your ability to take full advantage of that time. Whether it be for direction, freedom, power, balance, or any combination of reasons, effective planning can be the difference between accomplishing your goals and living a life of mediocrity. Don't just take my word for it, go out and ask the most successful people you know how important planning is.

When is the best time to start planning? Like the old adage about planting an oak tree, the answer is 20 years ago. However, the second best time is now! As the great Ben Franklin said, "If you fail to plan, then you are planning to fail." Heed the words of one of America's Founding Fathers, and start taking your life into your own hands. If you do not make a plan and take action, then you will inevitably be swept up into the plans of others. That is no way to live life. You only get one, and there is no reason to spend it any other way than you want to.

It doesn't matter who you are, where you come from, what resources or opportunities you have in front of you - none of that is going to change! We are dealt the hands that we are dealt. Are some people at an advantage? Sure, that's how the world works. That has nothing to do with how hard you work and the level to which you can reach if you plan. Nobody is going to do it for you, and if you continue to think that then you are going to live a life full of regret. You may think that my words are harsh, but they are the truth. The good news is that you can do it. There is not a single person on the planet that does not have the capacity to make their dreams a reality.

My final suggestion is to enjoy the journey. When you plan and take action to accomplish the goals that you set, you may end up achieving something completely different than what you set out to. What you learn about yourself and the world may be worth more to you than what you originally sought. If you keep planning and working, the world will unfold more opportunity to you than if you quit. Take opportunities that come your way, and before you know it you too can achieve greatness. And who knows, you might even have a little fun along the way.

www.ingramcontent.com/pod-product-compliance
Lightning Source LLC
Chambersburg PA
CBHW032258210326
41520CB00048B/5515